T0209322

Read Between The Signs
(Divine Signs)

Your Guide to Understanding Signs & Symbols

Lynnette Johnson-Terrien

BALBOA.PRESS
A DIVISION OF HAY HOUSE

Copyright © 2020 Lynnette Johnson-Terrien.

All rights reserved. No part of this book may be used or reproduced by
any means, graphic, electronic, or mechanical, including photocopying,
recording, taping or by any information storage retrieval system
without the written permission of the author except in the case of
brief quotations embodied in critical articles and reviews.

Balboa Press books may be ordered through booksellers or by contacting:

Balboa Press
A Division of Hay House
1663 Liberty Drive
Bloomington, IN 47403
www.balboapress.com
1 (877) 407-4847

Because of the dynamic nature of the Internet, any web addresses or
links contained in this book may have changed since publication and
may no longer be valid. The views expressed in this work are solely those
of the author and do not necessarily reflect the views of the publisher,
and the publisher hereby disclaims any responsibility for them.

The author of this book does not dispense medical advice or prescribe the use
of any technique as a form of treatment for physical, emotional, or medical
problems without the advice of a physician, either directly or indirectly. The
intent of the author is only to offer information of a general nature to help
you in your quest for emotional and spiritual well-being. In the event you use
any of the information in this book for yourself, which is your constitutional
right, the author and the publisher assume no responsibility for your actions.

Any people depicted in stock imagery provided by Getty Images are
models, and such images are being used for illustrative purposes only.
Certain stock imagery © Getty Images.

Print information available on the last page.

ISBN: 978-1-9822-4960-1 (sc)
ISBN: 978-1-9822-4962-5 (hc)
ISBN: 978-1-9822-4961-8 (e)

Library of Congress Control Number: 2020910770

Balboa Press rev. date: 06/22/2020

CONTENTS

ACKNOWLEDGMENTS

First and foremost, God, my Father.

The angels who woke me up in the middle of the night to whisper in my ear that I would do this project

My son, Prince Annan Koomson, whose monetary gift made this all possible.

My children, Lori, Paulie, and Paul "PJ," who put up with my moods and frustration.

For my late husband, whose love and confidence in me kept me going until he had to go home.

And last but certainly not least, Dr. Rick Weber, PsyD, who not only counseled my grief and depression but became my kindred soul. The more I opened up, the more he understood my life, spirituality, and the universal connection. He even marveled at my many signs. I thank him for being open so that I could be as well.

LJT

FOREWORD

As a scientist, the thought of Extrasensory Phenomena or paranormal activity took a backseat in my world of verifiable truth. My experience and education reminded me of the importance of reliable and valid proof of one's suppositions. In my early meetings with Lynnette Terrien, I was skeptical of her assertions that she received visitations from the afterlife. Her assertions suggested that her father, her mother, her sister, and her soul mate would make regular appearances in her day-to-day life. The orbs of light that would appear to her, spontaneous fragrances, and familiar objects were a few of the different ways that her significant others would show their presence to her.

At one point, I believe Lynnette sensed my disbelief, and she showed me my first glimpse of something that was otherworldly. Not being an expert with this type of phenomena, I was uncertain of what I should be looking for in her video. But after looking at the image for a brief moment it was evident there was a dancing light within her bedroom. With further investigation and slightly more of an open mind, I was able to see an image. Remarkably, it was the image of her soul mate, someone whom I knew fairly well. The details and outline of this apparition were astounding. I could make out his long beard and his kind eyes. My scientific mind shifted with this experience.

From that point forward, I became a believer in this phenomenon and acknowledged that Lynnette had a special ability to communicate with people from the afterlife. On several occasions over the last seven years, Lynnette has shared video images of spirits that have visited her within her home. She also has shared stories of other phenomena that would appear randomly in her life. After seeing so many pieces of evidence of their existence, I became a believer that this phenomenon is real. More important, I believe that Lynnette has the gift to take her experience with this and give it back to the world in a helpful and positive way.

This book is evidence that this phenomenon is real and has value for those willing to open their minds to the messages we receive from all realms of life. I have listened to the skeptics, and I do not believe that their counterarguments of photo doctoring or the presence of dust is what exists in Lynnette's experience. It is clear to me that she has a special gift and is capable of connecting to the other side. My assessment of her ability is based on her inherent goodness and the integrity of her character. Lynnette is trustworthy and truthful. This book is a testimonial to her gift and her ability to serve as a healer for others. There is a spiritual world that exists beyond our daily experience.

Richard P. Weber, PsyD
Licensed Clinical Psychologist

PREFACE

Growing up in Waukegan, Illinois, in the 1950s was the epitome of Middle America with one exception: my mother worked. I was always left in the loving hands of my aunt Hazel. I lived in an extended family home: my parents; my sister, Myra; me; my aunt; her daughter; and occasionally her son. My immediate family usually had the downstairs, and my aunt and her family had the upstairs. Therefore, I was never left alone and was well supervised. My sister, Myra, was ten years older than me, so she was a teenager in the 1950s, and her boyfriend, Jim, was a greaser: leather jacket, motorcycle, jet-black hair greased back, and very handsome. It was difficult being so much younger than her because I could not be her friend or her tagalong, although sometimes I was her tagalong because mom made her! That time in my life was great, our neighbors were friends or family, we all had best friends, and all our friends were family.

Waukegan during that time had a very small-town feel. We lived very close to downtown, and at Christmastime one could stand at the edge of town and look straight down, and the first thing one thought of was Bedford Falls. Unfortunately, not too many cities or towns have downtowns anymore, which of course was lost to progress. I think my fondest memories were walking up and down the streets or meeting my mom at the bus stop at Christmastime, and we would do our Christmas shopping up and down Genesee Street. Everything one needed was in those four to five blocks each way. The finest clothing stores, men's stores, shoe stores, five-and-dimes, pharmacies, hardware—it was all right there. And to my cousin's delight, one could get a racing form down there! Among the neighborhood kids, none of us were strangers to the A&P at the corner. We did more runs for more neighbors, but we also picked up pop bottles and took them back for the refund so we could buy candy. If I recall correctly, we didn't really walk anywhere; we ran. We ran to the store, ran to the dime store, and ran to the park. The only thing we didn't run to was school—unless we were late. We had the best parks in this town, and a lot of them, so we never wanted for a place to go. My favorite was Powell Park; it had the best hills, especially in the winter, and sledding down those hills was so much fun. There was also a band shell at the bottom of the hill, and local bands or orchestras would gladly put on shows there in the summertime. Families would go there with a picnic basket or a lunch bag and enjoy the entertainment under the stars.

I was generally a shy kid until one really got to know me, and then I wasn't shy at all. In my collection of friends—and there were many growing up—my best friend was my cousin Mary Jo, or MJ. She was one year, one month, and twenty-three days older than me. Because we were so close in age, our grandmother always dressed us alike. We were also both blonde. We went to Mary's parents' house quite often; Aunt Evelyn and my dad (her brother) were very close.

We had dinner there and played croquet. Daddy would bring freshly caught fish, and my aunt would cook it. When MJ and I were old enough to walk the two blocks from my house to the Genesee Theatre, we spent every Saturday there together; they had thirty-five-cent Saturday matinees.

We were always tagalongs with both of my aunts, my aunt Evelyn and her sister, Mama Hazel, when they went to the cemetery to visit Grandma's grave. We did not tell anyone for the longest time, but MJ and I got excited when we went to the cemetery because it was possibly the most peaceful place we had ever been; we also had a friend there. We had an angel who met us there every time we showed up. Keep in mind that MJ was about five and I was four, but we were so excited every time we saw him. Ascension Catholic Cemetery had the most beautiful statues scattered throughout. There was a statue of Christ and the little children with a square base, and that was where our angel would sit. The best way to describe him is about nine years old, blond pageboy hair, small wings, and not huge. He seemed to have a golden glow around him—not yellow or orange, just soft gold. After the first couple visits, we learned we had to stay back about fifteen feet, or he would leave. We never actually saw him speak, but we could hear him say hi or "I see you're back." Like I said, we were kids.

It wasn't too long after, when I was about five or six years old, that I had my first encounter with death. My twelve-year-old cousin Randy had drowned out in the Chain of Lakes. He was a beautiful child with red hair and freckles, and he was a sweet person. I remember attending his wake, looking at him, and thinking, *I don't want to be dead, and I don't want him to be dead either.* I think it was then that I began to obsess over my own death. My thoughts were that I would die. I would actually be alive in this nothingness, just black.

My mom was Pentecostal, and my dad was Lutheran. He left the religious raising of me up to my mom, so we attended a small church on a little side street in Waukegan. I will not denigrate anyone's religion or house of worship, but their way of worship frightened me, with the speaking in tongues and waving of the arms. I was young and very impressionable, and I pretty much resolved that I was going to go to hell.

To backtrack just a little, when I was about three years old, I was very sick. They had no idea what was wrong with me. I was in a coma, and they were not giving my parents much hope that I was going to come out of the coma or survive. My aunt Evelyn, a devout

Catholic, talked to my dad, and he agreed to have me baptized Catholic. She got in touch with her parish priest and told him what was going on and how sick I was. Right then, we needed divine intervention as well as divine healing. This was 1954, maybe 1955, and here came Father Cull with everything necessary for a proper baptism. He was in full regalia along with his bag of candles, oils, and holy water. Now, mind you, I was in a coma. The priest chanted in Latin and set up everything on the hospital table—the vials of oils, water, and stoles—with everything precise. At the moment all the candles were lit, I opened my eyes and said, "Are we having a happy birthday?" Divine healing? I do believe!

When I was old enough, it was not necessary to convert; I simply took on my Catholic faith, and I made my first confession, first communion, and confirmation. I was married in the church.

I found that with Catholicism, there was more spirituality involved with this faith. There were saints and angels and archangels, and this intrigued me. Of course, it wasn't until sometime later in my life that I would pursue this as a career, but before I began educating, things had already started happening in my life. It didn't take me long to realize that these were signs that things were okay on the other side. I'm not a medium, and I am not a psychic. I would describe myself more as an empath. I know when a spirit is near, and I know who it is, but I have not evolved enough or become enlightened enough. The majority of my dealings are with family members or friends. Although I continue to learn and evolve and hopefully become more enlightened, I will be able to do and understand more. But for now, I'm quite happy knowing those I love are okay and that they show up on a regular basis. I know I'm never alone, I know I'm protected, and I know I'm loved by all from the other side.

CHAPTER 1

I was raised by the two greatest influences in my life, my father and my aunt, whom I called Mama Hazel. I could talk about anything with them. We got into discussions of death or visions because I was interested in them, although I was still very afraid of death and I was still quite young. I hadn't pursued my Catholic faith yet, so pretty much the only reference I had was the Pentecostal teachings. My father was a very simple man with simple wants and needs, but he was quite knowledgeable and we would discuss things of a supernatural nature. It wasn't always spiritual either.

When I was about eleven my cousin David and his friend Wally were beating on our door just about in hysterics. Both had been crying, and these were grown men. Why would they be crying? They said, "Please let us in, just please let us in." This was two o'clock in the morning! My mom let them in, put on a pot of coffee, and sat with them to try to calm their nerves. My cousin was a former marine, so it took a lot to scare him, but what happened this night shook him to his soul. He told us that he and Wally had had their girlfriends over to the apartment, and they had cooked some pizzas and were hanging out. At about twelve thirty, he said the room got very cold. They were all in the living room, and it was like the temperature had dropped thirty degrees. He didn't know what to think, and then the lights flickered and went dim. He said it was then that he started looking around the room, and up in the corner by the ceiling, where the ceiling and the wall met, he saw it: a pair of angel's wings, hovering. No angel, just a pair of glowing angel's wings. This man had a strange sense of humor at best and had mocked God on many occasions. Therefore, I could understand the fear that this vision had put into him. I had never seen this man in such a state of fear. He was trembling, crying, and agitated. It was heartbreaking, but it was also a bit unnerving. Years later, when he was dying, he had a more positive view on God and the hereafter, and I believe he made his peace. He did tell my sister that when he was having a heart attack, a giant hand came down out of the sky reaching for him, and he said, "I always felt that if I had reached for that hand, I would go to heaven. Now I wonder whether I will make it." My sister was quick to point out that he had had an option to go with that time or stay because his suffering was great. She said that she did believe God gave him an option, and I am quite sure that he did indeed go to heaven.

Shortly after this, I experienced two deaths that would impact my life for a long time to come. On November 22, 1963, while heading to gym class, our teacher stopped us in single file to inform us that President John F. Kennedy had been killed in Dallas. Being preteenage girls, of course we were all in love with John Kennedy, but we also thought he was a good man and a good president. Many girls broke down in tears, and one could even see some of the guys' faces turn red as their eyes filled with tears. This was an assassination! Someone killed the man holding the highest office in the world. How could this happen? For the next few days, I lay on the floor in front of the television and watched as the rest of the world did, and many things played out. I was horrified when I saw Lee Harvey Oswald shot and killed while being taken out of the Dallas police station. My heart also broke as I watched a bloodied Jackie and Bobby Kennedy with the casket at the air force base. Over the next few days, I watched our late president lie in state in the rotunda of the Capitol. I watched the throngs of people pay homage to him. I felt that the caisson carrying his casket was most appropriate not only for a president but for a war hero. A staunch but shaky Jackie stood there with her children, and John Junior saluted his father as he went by. This was not only heartbreaking, but I felt put us on shaky ground because we were still in the middle of the Cold War. Where would Lyndon Johnson take us?

After all the grieving and turmoil of the president's funeral, things started to calm down, and we began looking forward to Christmas. It hadn't snowed much, but I do remember the night of December 7, 1963. It was the worst fog I have ever seen; I couldn't see my hand in front of my face. That night took my brother-in-law. The fog was so intense, and he, his friend Dickie, and a young lady named Connie were driving down old Townline Road, a dark, dirt back road with no lights to guide the way. There was a train track, but it did not have signal horns, and flashing lights could not be seen because of the fog. Of course, Jim was driving very fast, and there being no horns they didn't see the train when they hit it at a high rate of speed. Jim and Dickie were killed instantly, however authorities believe the young lady lived for a while after the accident. This was the closest person to me to die so far, and I had a great deal of trouble getting over Jim's death. He was always like a big brother. Every time I looked at my two nieces, I thought of him, and I can honestly say I cried for a year.

I remember my dad telling me that things happen in threes. For example, three knocks on a door and there is no one there means someone is going to die. It could be anything that came in the succession of three. My sister was feeding my niece, who was in a highchair, and there was a string of those big plastic bells hanging on the side of the highchair. My mom was toward the front of the house in the living room, and she said that she heard three knocks at the door, but there was no one there. She didn't think anything of it, but then the bells on my niece's highchair rang three times! Nobody was playing with them or touching them, but they rang three times in a row. A couple of hours later, my sister got a phone call from Oklahoma that her natural father, Earl, had died of a heart attack.

I was in my midtwenties when I started to have the dreams my dad had told me about. First, Mama Hazel came down one night and told her daughter Donna, "I think you should go see your dad at the hospital tomorrow." Donna asked why. "I was just upstairs getting the kids settled down, and she said, 'In my ear I heard three breaths, one right after the other.' You know what that means, so you'd better go see your dad before something happens." The next day, however, Mama Hazel had a stroke and was taken by ambulance to the hospital. They needed to do some testing to see what was causing the stroke. They did an angiogram, which could be a very dangerous test at that time. When they shot the dye into her artery, she started having several small strokes because the injection of the dye was breaking off plaque in her arteries and sending it to her brain. She went into a coma after several strokes. I believe it was about three days of her being in intensive care that I dreamed that I was walking through Washington Park in Waukegan, and there was a black dog and a white dog fighting. In the dream, I saw Hazel's children, Donna and Ronnie, walking on the other side of the park. I yelled at them to please stop these dogs from fighting, but they looked at me and let the dogs go ahead and fight. The next day, my aunt took a turn for the worse, and at about midnight on the night of October 18, she crossed over. The breaths she had heard were for herself.

A couple of weeks after her mom's funeral, my cousin Donna was cleaning her house, and she had a small dining area that was hardwood floor. She waxed it on her hands and knees and then went into the kitchen to let it dry. She grabbed a cup of coffee, went back into the dining room after the wax had dried, and sat down to take a breather. As she was taking a sip of coffee, she noticed something on the floor that she had just waxed, which was sparkling clean. How could something have gotten there so soon? She was home alone. She walked over and bent down to pick it up, and she froze on the spot. It was her mother's cloth eyeglass chain. Obviously shaken, she called her brother at work and said, "Please stop by on your way home." When he arrived around three o'clock, she showed him her findings.

He said, "Call the funeral home and ask them if they sent this home."

She called them, and they told her, no, the eyeglass chain was checked off as being incinerated with her other belongings. Donna then asked how that was possible when she was standing there holding the chain. The funeral director told her, "I do get these kind of calls from time to time."

The following April, I had a similar dream. I don't recall it being the same place, but it was two dogs, one black and one white, fighting. It was my husband and I watching them, standing nearby, and no one else was in the dream. That night, we went out to dinner, and I told my husband, Paul, "I think my dad is going to die." He asked me why I thought that, so I told him of my dream and said, "You know Daddy's been sick a long time." After a stroke in 1969, he had been wheelchair-bound for quite some time. Along with his chain-smoking habit, of course he had emphysema, so it was my assumption that it would be my dad.

After we got back home, my husband's parents stopped by. They never stayed long because my father-in-law was so impatient. They stayed long enough for Pa to have a drink, play with the kids a bit, and head out. When they got home, they gave us a call and said that they were at the stop light at Glen Rock and Jackson when they were rear-ended by a man apparently not paying attention. The jolt pushed them through the stoplight a little bit, and my father-in-law hit the steering wheel. He said he was fine and a little sore, but he added, "I'm madder than hell. I'm not as hurt as I am mad." Typical feisty little guy. There was some damage to his car, and he was going to take it the next day in have it looked at.

At about five thirty the next morning, we get a phone call from my mother-in-law. They had taken my father-in-law to the hospital with what they believed was a heart attack. He had been throwing up and chest pains. My husband said, "I will meet you there in ten minutes." He was gone about an hour and a half, and when he came in the door, I knew. He said, "He's gone." So you see? The dream wasn't for my dad—it was for my husband's.

✿

CHAPTER 2

I mentioned earlier that my father had a stroke in 1969 He had been not only my parent but my hero my friend, and my nurturer. He was an incredible man who raised me from the time I was twelve years old until his stroke when I was sixteen. Although I have a sister, we were half sisters (we had the same mother but different fathers). My dad loved her as much as he loved me, and we were not raised any differently. But I think I fit the bill for both a daughter and a son because I learned to play softball, baseball, and poker, and I was a poker dealer for their Saturday night penny ante poker games. That was at the age of six. He wanted so much for me—in fact, he wanted everything for me. I remember he came home one day so proud. He had bought me a teeter totter, and it went up and down and around and around. However, it was difficult to operate that toy as the only kid around.

Never wanting to disappoint me, my dad would come out and would take his hand and teeter me up and down.

Dad had been a commercial fisherman when he reached the age to work. My grandfather had fishing boats up on Washington Island, Wisconsin, and when my dad moved to Waukegan, he continued commercial fishing for Mathon's Restaurant. He did this for several years, and believe it or not, he could not swim a stroke, so when he was offered a good job at the Lake County Courthouse, he gladly accepted. Commercial fishermen will tell you it's a rough job. He still loved to fish, and at the age of five, I was digging night crawlers at five o'clock in the morning. Then he would tie me with rope to the pier, and we fished. I caught fish with my little cane pole because I couldn't handle the reel, but I caught enough to make him proud of me. I can't put on paper what this man meant to me. With my sister being ten years older, when I was six, she was sixteen and married, and she had a daughter. My dad did everything to keep me occupied and to make me happy. But he also loved my sister, and he did his best to make her happy. He adored her children, so there was never "his daughter" or "my daughter"—it was us! He loved kids and animals. As a very patient man with a huge heart, he would literally give the shirt off his back to help out someone. I have seen him go without so that others would have things such as food or a place to live. He was a very giving man, and he instilled some pretty good morals in this girl. Until the day he died, I called him Daddy.

I had married quite young, and I did care about him of course, but I also think I felt like I was a burden to my dad, and he didn't have a life. I thought if I got married, I'd be less of a burden We had been living in a two flat, and my dad had the upstairs. When my cousin and her family moved out, my husband and I took the downstairs. In a few months, we had a baby coming and needed another bedroom, so we found a huge house on the corner. Consequently, both fathers came to live with us. My husband's father had walked with a cane for years, so we always knew when he was coming from his room upstairs because we would hear three footsteps: right, left, and cane. Shortly before my father's stroke, Bill died of a heart attack in his car. Unfortunately, my husband found him—something I did not foresee or feel. It wasn't until after his death that things started popping. With my father in the hospital with the stroke and Bill gone, it was just my husband, me, and our six-month-old daughter in this huge, old Victorian house.

While lying in bed one night, I heard the three footsteps: right, left, cane. I wasn't going to open my mouth, but my husband said, "Do you hear the old man walking?" All I could do was shake my head. We could clearly hear him walk from his room upstairs to the living room, the sitting room, and the dining room. We heard the chair pull out where he always sat. The next morning when we got up, the chair where Bill usually sat was still pulled out from the night before. This went on until we separated and both moved out. There were many not-so-friendly events that took place in this house, but maybe that's for another time and another book.

My dad suffered the stroke at my house, at the kitchen table. I had a little girl six months old, and he was in his glory with her. Watching him experience the occurrence of the stroke was difficult for me to handle. We got him to the hospital by ambulance, and they put me off in a room somewhere and said someone would be with me shortly. Not thinking, I sent him to one hospital, and my sister worked at the other hospital. He had always gone to the hospital that I took him to, and I assumed all his records would be there. My sister met me there, and by this time I was half crazy because nobody had come to tell me anything. By the time my sister got there, they said, "Oh, Mr. Johnson is in a room." My sister, her husband, and I all got on the elevator, went up, and found his room. He was sitting up and quite jovial, talking and interacting. We were so relieved to see him in such good spirits. We stayed with him a while, they took his vitals, and everything was fine. We went home for the night. I didn't have a phone at the time; it was a luxury then.

My sister showed up the next morning at my house seeming quite rattled. "We have to get to the hospital right away—something's happened to Pa." Apparently, he had suffered a couple more strokes in the night, which we discovered later were caused by a blood clot on the brain. Again, this was 1969 and they didn't have technology to stop the damage as they do now. When we got to the hospital, he was in a coma. We took turns during the day. One of us visited, and one would go get lunch or whatever. At night we took the two chairs and two blankets and curled up next to his bed because we were going nowhere. My sister did have to go to work, so I would stay with him. He had very bad bronchitis, so I stayed in the room so I could suction him whenever he needed it, and I washed him up. My aunts Evelyn and Hazel came up and would sit with me. Thank goodness for my aunt Evelyn because I was broke and hungry, and she bought me lunch. She couldn't believe someone who weighed eighty pounds could eat so much! The doctors and nurses said that he could hear me, so I talked to him about everything: the weather, my daughter, my hair, the snow—whatever came to mind, I carried on a conversation about it.

Thankfully, on the third day, he came out of the coma. However, he was not unscathed. He had suffered permanent paralysis on the left side. He would need physical therapy and a wheelchair. This was so much for me to take in at sixteen years old. He stayed as an inpatient at that hospital for about two months, and then he was transferred to the county hospital, where it was decided, against my fits of stomping and screaming, that he would need to go to a nursing home. As impossible as I knew it was, I wanted to take him home to live with me; obviously I was not being very realistic. As soon as he was well enough to sit in a wheelchair unattended, he was moved to a nursing home. I lost so much sleep and so many tears because I was unable to give back to him what he had given to me. The stroke changed him some too: he became frustrated and cranky, but then he would get emotional just as quickly. The physical therapy was very painful, and he had been in a bed for so long that his leg had started to atrophy. He could lift it up but not straighten it out, and we could see that walking was not in his near future. My three children knew him only in a wheelchair, but they loved him, and that didn't matter. Whoever got there first got his lap and the first ride in the wheelchair. They would kiss him, hug him, and tickle him, and he loved every minute. The first few years for holidays and such, we went to my sister's house because I didn't have a house yet; I had a small apartment, so it was easier to go to her big house for the holidays.

CHAPTER 3

In 1981, my dad was in a nursing home that I was not at all fond of, and we had a house in which I knew I could handle him. I had three children aged twelve, nine, and seven, and I knew they wouldn't mind helping me with Papa at all. One day that facility angered me so much that I called them and told them that I would be there in thirty minutes, so they should have him in the lobby with all of his belongings, all of his money, and a list of his accounts. I would be there to get him.

It was great to have Daddy with me. I enjoyed cooking for him and talking with him. He had a little TV he watched his own shows on, so he didn't have to worry about coming down the stairs in his wheelchair to the TV room. It was difficult to transport wheelchairs back then because they didn't have the hydraulic lift vans and buses as they do now, so everywhere I had to take him, I had to transfer him from his wheelchair into my car and vice versa. I managed to drop him one day, and we both got the giggles so much that we sat down in the grass, laughing.

On July 15, when he was having his coffee in the morning, he said, "You know, Dolly (his nickname for me), I am not going to live to see the weekend."

I said, "Daddy, please don't talk like that. I love you, and you are going to be here for a long time."

He looked at me and said, "I have to tell you what happened last night. After I got in bed and lay down, I didn't have a coughing fit. However, I was hovering above the bed, breathing just fine and watching myself on the bed." This kind of rattled my constitution at the moment. I knew what he was saying, and I knew he was more than likely right. The next day on the sixteenth, he had to go over to the hospital for some tests the doctor had ordered, so I transferred him into my car and got the testing done. On the way back, we stopped at Shirl's, who had the best ice cream anywhere. We each got a cone and an extra one for my aunt, and then we drove a little fast the four blocks to her house so it wouldn't melt. She saw us pull into the driveway and met us outside.

She was standing on Daddy's side of the car and said the strangest thing: "I was sitting in the living room today and saw three flashes of light go past my front window." Knowing what the three of anything could mean, my dad looked at my aunt and said, "Maybe it's Stanley." Stanley was his brother, my uncle, who had cancer at the time.

Aunt Evelyn said, "You're probably right, Buster. He hasn't been doing so good lately. Maybe I'll give them a call tonight before I go to bed."

We finished our ice cream, and Daddy was tired and wanted to go home to take his nap, before dinner and *The Six Million Dollar Man* started. That night I made one of his favorites: Polish sausage, sauerkraut, and potatoes. He ate so heartily, and that always made me feel good. He watched a little TV, and then as per his nightly routine, he had one shot of brandy and went to bed.

The next morning, I was in the bathroom right across the hall from my dad's room, getting ready for work. I heard him holler for me. "Dolly, Dolly, come here. I can't breathe."

I dropped my makeup in the sink and dashed the five feet to his doorway. He was sitting on the side of the bed, shaking and having great difficulty breathing. I asked if he had taken his breathing medicine, and he said yes. I asked him if he wanted another breathing pill, and he agreed to that. He hated ambulances, but I did ask him, "Daddy, can I call the ambulance, at least for them to bring you some oxygen?" "Okay, Dolly, we can do that?." I called the ambulance and they were there in no time. My oldest daughter and my son, the youngest, were home with me, and they were quite unnerved when the ambulance arrived. I called my aunt and told her that they would be taking him to the hospital because he was having a heart attack. They were in the bedroom working on him, and I went to the doorway and looked at him. I said, "I love you, Daddy." He was lying down and gave his usual reply: "Me too." Then he lay down and died. So you see, he was right because it was Friday morning—he didn't make it to the weekend. When my aunt told us of her three flashes of light, they immediately thought of my uncle, but in fact it was my dad.

My husband wanted to take us all out for dinner that night because I was such a wreck, but I declined. I wanted some time by myself; I simply wanted to be alone. After they left, I walked into our big sitting room with the fireplace. There was no noise and no TV. Suddenly I had this incredibly strong smell of Aunt Hazel's perfume. It got strong enough to make my eyes water, and then I got very calm and flopped on the couch. I realized she was letting me know they were together.

That night while lying in bed, even with three kids and my husband, it seemed so empty. Daddy's wheelchair was folded up and sat in the corner of the living room. His TV had not been turned on all day; I guess no one wanted to bother it. That night while in bed, we were wide awake when outside our bedroom door, and I heard the brakes on my dad's wheelchair. My husband said, "Did you just hear that?" I said yes. "What did you hear?" I replied, "The brakes on my dad's chair." "So you know he never left you." Then the tears really started.

CHAPTER 4

A couple of weeks after my dad died, I had been on a major hunt for my glasses. I was prone to losing them on top of my head, at the bottom of my purse, or in the bathroom after putting on my makeup. I never put them in anything such as a cabinet or in a drawer. It took about three days of hunting and searching, and still nothing. I had a little telephone table that held the telephone and a small drawer for the phone book. I never really used the phone book because at that time, 411 was free. But for some reason, while sitting there, I opened the drawer to grab the phone book, and there were my glasses. I never went in that drawer for any good given reason, yet there they were. Instinctively I said out loud, "Thank you, Daddy." From that day, on his pranks continued.

About ten months after my dad's death, we packed up everything and headed for Texas. My husband had a job offer, and I was tired of the Chicago winters. We had a small, two-bedroom house on a nice, quiet street. We were settling in, and the kids were making friends. The second week we were there, I had a vivid dream. I was watching my dad in his wheelchair in the aisle of an airplane; he was relaxed, happy, and telling the flight attendant that his daughter had moved to Texas, and he was going there to live with her. Now, my dad was afraid to stand on a thick rug, let alone get into an airplane, but that was my dream, and I never underestimate my dreams.

The next day, I had some errands to run, and when I got home and opened the door of my house, this odor hit me in the face like a brick! It was the smell of the last nursing home my dad had been in. I sat down in the nearest chair and knew that my dream was real, that he was here. It was an unmistakable smell. That afternoon when my kids got home from school, my daughter Pookie went to her room to finish unpacking her stuff that had arrived the day before. The minute she opened her suitcase, she got the same smell. She was pretty rattled when she came out to tell me what had happened. When I told her of my experience earlier in the day, she sat next to me and asked, "Do you really think Papa is here with us?" I nodded yes because I was certain that he had made his way to be with me and my kids.

We had the experiences of things being moved from one place to another or not being there, but when you went back, there it was. I failed to mention earlier that my dad had a great sense of humor, so these pranks were up his alley. My children took great delight in knowing that Papa was with them. These experiences seemed to take away the grief they had been feeling since his crossing.

Things did not work out in Texas, so a few months later, we were on a Greyhound bus back to Waukegan. It was an experience, to say the least. When we arrived in Chicago, we didn't have two dimes to rub together, but we had something much better: our faith. That faith held us through some harrowing experiences. First, the five of us bunking in with my niece and her young son in a one-bedroom apartment. Thank God my kids had friends to stay with on and off, we still had to find jobs and get a car We had to start all over with very little belongings. We then had an opportunity to take over a restaurant that was in the process of being purchased, but it was still in limbo, so we ended up living in a motel of the owner's. The five of us in one room, and two beds! My husband would work the front desk, and I folded laundry all day. In a couple of months, we were in a kitchenette type room at the hotel where we were managing the restaurant. It was a little bigger, but we were still stacked on top of each other.

This period in our lives got us through to where we were meant to be, a three-bedroom house and reasonable rent. We grabbed it right away. It is that house we still have today. Our children grew up there and made their lifelong friends in the neighborhood, and now we run a business out of that house. We lived in that house about two years before we bought it, and we have been there thirty-nine years.

My dad seemed to be most comfortable at this house after we had finally settled down and weren't living like gypsies anymore. We had finally established ourselves as a family. The kids went to Catholic school, I was working at a good job at a local hospital, and my husband had his own little taxi company, which later turned into a

Medi-Van company that we owned until his passing, transporting people in wheelchairs or those who have no transportation to doctors' appointments. The kids were happy, we were happy, and things started to settle down as family life.

I hate to assume anything, but I'm pretty sure that Daddy rode back on that Greyhound bus with us because he made himself right at home in this house. It wasn't long before things started getting moved, disappearing, and reappearing. It was so often that the children came up with "Papa's a poltergeist." They loved it when they were missing something and couldn't find it; they would stand there and say, "Papa, where is it?"

My husband was going to culinary school on his GI Bill, and he had awesome tools that he worked with. He brought them home every night so as to keep track of them. His big carving knife went missing somewhere around October, and we tore apart the kitchen. We pulled out every drawer, cleaned out every cabinet, and looked through kitchen linens for months trying to find this knife. On March 5, my husband opened the drawer where he normally had his expensive carving knife, and there it lay right on top in the drawer. It didn't seem too hard to figure out who had taken this and made a game of it, because March 5 was my daddy's birthday! The next item to disappear was Paul's egg pan. No one touched the egg pan! That thing, which hung in the pantry for years and years, was suddenly MIA, no longer hanging in the pantry. We went through the same routine as we did with the knife. Paul got so frustrated that he bought a new pan. My dad must have a thing with numbers because on December 12, Paul opened the pantry door, and there on the hook was his old egg pan. It was Paul's birthday!!!

One event that sticks out in my daughter's mind is her Young Authors story that she had to do for school. She was doing her story on my dad. She had done an excellent job on it so far, and the night before she was to turn it in, she was tweaking it when I called her in for dinner. After dinner, she dashed back to her room so she could get it perfect to turn it in the next day. It was not there. It wasn't anywhere. I asked her, "Where exactly did you leave it?" "Right here in the blue folder, on top of all my books on my bed. The folder is gone!" Living with "Papa the poltergeist" was like having a constant Easter egg hunt at my house. We were always looking for something, and that night was no different. We went through every piece of paper that she had in folders, went through her books, and took all the blankets and sheets off her bed. She was getting very frustrated and scared that she would not have the story to turn in the next day; she had worked so hard on it. She went in the kitchen in tears and said, "Papa, I need that story. If you put it back, I bet I could get an A on it." She headed back to her bedroom, which was right off the kitchen.

I heard her yell, "Papa!" I went in her room to see her sitting on the bed, smiling from ear to ear with tears in her eyes, and holding her story. I shook my head and asked her where it was. "Right here on top of everything, Mom, like it had never been moved." I said, "Then why are you crying?"

"Because I know it truly was Papa." The story was not only about my dad but also about "Papa the poltergeist," and yes, she got an A.

It was not uncommon to walk through my house and hear my kids talking to Papa. They had found that by talking to him, they had a confidant whom they could tell anything to and wouldn't rat them out. He probably holds more secrets of my kids on the other side than I can imagine. Many times I would walk by a bedroom and hear, "Papa, do you think Mom would …?" or, "Papa, you are not going to believe this!" I never lingered as to hear the rest because I felt that was intruding or eavesdropping, and that was their time. I was so happy that they felt they could sit in their room by themselves and talk to Papa, so I didn't interfere.

One day after the kids had gone off to school, I decided to take a breather from housework. I sat down and turned on Maury Povich, and his guest that day was a psychic medium by the name of Rosemary Altea. I watched this woman, absolutely mesmerized; she was the real deal. She described the people who were talking from the other side, and she was so specific. Then she explained that she had two books out, and they were the first two things on my Christmas list. After that, I read every word she ever wrote and listened to every CD she recorded. I was so voracious about the information I could obtain from this woman. I got the CD collection of You Own the Power, and I went to sleep every night listening to these CDs. I practiced and practiced, and I did everything she said to do on the CD: meditating, visualizing, focusing, and learning to hone my senses.

She was, best put, my first teacher, and the many things that I learned from her written and spoken words were invaluable. We can all be open to the other side if we free up our cluttered mind and noise and be open to God and willing to listen. As I said, I am not a medium; I am at best a "sensitive." This did not happen because I saw Rosemary on the TV show—it was years of believing, thinking, and having life experiences and signs from the other side. I can feel when a spirit is with me, and I know who this spirit is.

I have also learned from very evolved mediums to always protect myself. I pray, I surround myself with the white light of Christ, and I ask my guardian angels for their protection and safety. I've also learned that people who lead negative lives or who thrive in negative energies can bring this into my home and into my life. Therefore, I've learned to cleanse by saging, also known as smudging, my home. For example, if someone comes into my home that has perhaps been in prison or lived in the lower dregs of life, for every person they associated with, they took with them some of their negative energy. They are also carrying their own negative energy, so when they come into my home, they could be carrying the energy of an entire prison cell block. I smudge and cleanse and holy water everything as soon as they are off my property. I certainly don't need malingerers. If you don't cleanse, you may find your life a little topsy-turvy. Maybe you cut yourself, or you slip and break an ankle. You can count on the fact that the negative energy probably had more than just a little to do with this. If you have pets, I can promise you they will warn you of the negative energy. I have a little Maltapoo, Phoebe. One afternoon, a friend of my cousin stopped by. This little dog went crazy. The phrase "If your dog doesn't like someone, you probably shouldn't either" is true! I have never seen Phoebe in such a state. She's not a vicious dog—she's a sweet, loving, little lapdog. But she was having no part of this man and was acting crazy; she was attacking and shaking, and her hackles were up. A few months later, he was arrested for having robbed several banks, and he had been in prison for molestation. If you are iffy on your instincts, trust your pets'!

Before I get into the depth of the book regarding the signs from the other side, I want to warn you of one more thing: the Ouija board. Never bring one into your home! It is the epitome of negative energy. When my children were preteens, they were playing with it (but I'm sure they were pushing the pointer). One day my two daughters, Lori and Paulie (Pookie), were playing with the Ouija board, and all of a sudden we heard this incredibly loud, gutteral growl. The pointer started shooting all over the board. The girls took their hands off of it, and it shot across the board and fell off onto the floor. I grabbed that Ouija board, cracked it across my knee, took it to the garbage, and threw it in the trash. Later that day, Pookie and my son PJ took it to the garage and burned it. I had two terrified girls, and never again have they touched a Ouija board.

CHAPTER 5

My oldest daughter, Lori, married a young man by the name of Delfino; he was called either Chino or Fino. I called this young man my gentle giant because he was six feet five inches, was about 250 pounds, and was the sweetest man I have ever known. He had bad luck, but I know that we all have to go through things for a reason, and how we handle it is how we evolve spiritually. When he was three, he was hit by a car, which affected his speech: he spoke slow and precise. He didn't believe in violence, he adored, my daughter, and she loved him. When he was about nineteen years old, he was falsely accused of a gang rape. He spent about two years in the county jail before the woman recanted that he was involved in any way. However, this was something that wasn't going to go away overnight. He had to register as a sex offender even though the victim recanted his involvement.

A few years later, in the neighborhood where he lived, he made friends with everyone, but one particular man took a liking to Fino and told him, "You can borrow my lawn mower or my snow blower whenever you need to; the shed's usually open." One day Fino did borrow the lawn mower, and when the owner got home, he thought, *Where is my lawnmower?* Not thinking, he called the police and thought his shed had been vandalized. When Fino saw the police, he went down there to let them know he had the lawn mower. I guess I should add that Fino is Hispanic. Well, his neighbor was fine with that, Fino brought back the lawn mower, and everything was right with the world—except for the police, who handcuffed him, threw them in the squad car, and took him to jail for breaking, entering, and stealing. This giant of a man never hurt anyone. His neighbor testified on his behalf over this incident, but Fino was still given eighteen months in county jail.

A few years later, we learned that Fino had lupus. This can be a very tricky disease, mainly because you're on blood thinners and must watch what you eat and have your blood tested. It requires certain medications, and you cannot have certain foods. Even with all that went on in his life, he called me every day at lunchtime. "Hi, Ma, whatcha doing?" When he was thirty years old, he was in Chicago visiting his dad, and he walked to a bus stop probably close to midnight. As he stood there, he was approached by six gang members and they looked ready to pounce as they surrounded him. As nonviolent as he was, the odds weren't very good. He tried to run, but they shot him in the back. Then he grabbed the gun and shot one of them. He never knew whether he hit him, killed him, or what. It took six of them to bring him down, and they beat him with chains, stomped him with boots, stabbed him, cut the tips of his fingers off his right hand, gouged out an eye, and left him in the street for dead. About three hours later, a neighbor finally called police as a bus was coming up. Fino said he remembers them saying, "This guy's not gonna make it."

His mother told me when she got to the emergency room at Mount Sinai Hospital in Chicago, one couldn't tell that his face was indeed a human face. When I saw him three days later, I could not believe it. I could not believe what they had done to this fine young man. He did tell me that while he was in the emergency room, he was kind of floating around the room, and when he looked back toward the opening of the curtain, he saw his deceased sister Bina standing there with a whole carnival behind her. She shook her head at him as if to say, "No, you're not coming." He survived this, I made sure he got an artificial eye and it looked like its own. Later, his friends came to him and said they were going to go to Chicago and take care of this. Fino said, "No, you are not. The violence stops right here." He had been staying with his mom while recuperating, and she up and moved him to Chicago. We knew nothing about it—he was simply gone. He would call me at lunchtime and say, "I'm afraid to go out. I just sit here and look out the window." I miss you and Lori, Mom. I hate Chicago. I'll never like it after what happened."

A couple months later we got a phone call that he was taken to the hospital in the middle of the night. His lupus was very bad. I don't know whether he wasn't taking his medication right or things were simply working against him. While he was in the hospital, I believe at University of Chicago, he had a few strokes, and his kidneys shut down. My friend and I went to see him, and he was improving. When I walked out of that room, he said, "Hey, Ma, I love you."

I said, "I love you too, Fino."

Because he was improving, they moved him to a hospital where they would wean him off the ventilator. Such horror stories come out of that hospital from Fino and his mom. They told her she couldn't transfer him to a better hospital because then she would be charged with his murder; she wasn't really up on all the legalities of certain things, so it scared her. Fino also told us that one male nurse at night had slapped him once and held a pillow over his face. His mom called my daughter and me to come up on a Sunday afternoon, October 3, 1999. This hospital was creepy. There was a receptionist and no one else on the main floor; we heard no overhead pages. We asked directions to the unit he was in, and she told us to go to the second floor and turn left. We got to the second floor and turned right instead of left. All the doors down that hall were locked, and the hallway was dark. We went back the other way, and up to a tiny unit with possibly four patients in it, all the doors were all locked. That was all that was functioning in this "hospital."

My son-in-law crossed from this life to the other side at 12:54 p.m. To this day, between 12:00 and 1:00 p.m., I get a phone call where there's no one there, and the caller ID says it's out of area. I know full well who's on the other end of that phone. I wrote a letter that the priest read at his funeral. Basically I said that I knew Fino's time here on earth was not shortened; his work was done and I truly believe that his work was to teach us. In his thirty-one years, he taught so many people forgiveness, compassion, empathy, and unconditional love. I miss him, but I know he's with me every single day

CHAPTER 6

After Fino's death, I took to reading and rereading everything Rosemary Altea put out there because I knew somehow that he was still with me. I wanted to know more, and I wanted to know whether there was a way I could do this. Could I channel? Could I communicate? I had moved out of our house and into a place of my own, so when I wasn't working, I was devoting my time to the exercises Rosemary offered in her CDs. The first thing I was able to take away from this was that concentration is very important. As I said, I am not a medium; I am a light worker and an empath, which means I feel things. I can sense when spirits around. I also have the ability to capture a family spirit on film in the shape of orbs, which I will get into later. This has solidified my belief that they are still with us! I have a photograph of an orb

I zoomed in on, and it is clearly my sister's face. Another one is the face of my dalmatian!

A few years after moving into my little hideaway here, a dear friend of mine passed away at the age of forty-four. He crossed on Sweetest Day, September 13. We had worked together and had gone out a couple of times for fun, and he was such a nice young man who had demons of his own. We talked about them, so I was very shocked to read of his death. I went to his memorial service and spoke about working with him, noting how we used to tease him because he blushed so easily. Three days later, when I came in the door from work, there was a penny lying on the floor, and I picked it up and looked at it. When I did, I immediately got the sensation of spirit, and on closer examination, I noticed that it was a 1944 D Penny. Sometimes you have to pull the curtain away to find the sign. I immediately noticed the "44." The entire year had nothing to do with me or him, but he was forty-four years old when he crossed. And the D series? His name was Dan! Right away I ran to the computer, got on Rosemary Altea's community forum, and put this all out there. I got plenty of feedback: Of course he's trying to contact you, of course he's letting you know that he's with you!

A couple weeks later, I was doing laundry, taking everything out of the hamper, and sorting by color when I heard some change. Everything was out of the hamper, and there are at the bottom lay a dime and three pennies. Thirteen cents. Remember that Dan died on September 13. Once again I hit that forum, and everybody agreed that I was getting signs from a friend and that he was letting me know of his presence. As soon as I saw that money, I got the spirit bumps and knew he was here. I smiled and said, "Thanks, Dan."

These are the types of signs that you have to scratch your head and take a second look at, because it does have a meaning, and you are the only one for whom it's going to have a meaning. To the average person, a 1944 penny probably wouldn't have meant much. I had to note his age, not that he was born that year. Nothing in that year had anything to do with him but his age. And immediately when I saw the D series on the penny and got spirit bumps everywhere, I knew what it meant: my friend had contacted me. Then the thirteen cents on the day of his death the thirteenth. Many people overthink the signs, and many miss them as well. Don't seek them out; they will be there. They generally appear out of the blue. I'm putting all this down on paper because I want people to know what the signs are that they are getting from their loved ones. I don't want them to feel that their loved ones are not getting in touch with them. I don't want people to walk with their heads down, looking for pennies or going through pockets in the hopes of finding twenty-seven cents. I want you to know that when the sign is there, it's there for you, and you will know the meaning behind it and whom it is from.

I'll give you one of my best instances. Spirit has a way of getting a song that is tuned to you, or song or a commercial that means something to you. I see commercials way late at night that pertained to a private joke between me and one of my dearest loves ("Bubba"), and I know when that plays, it is him. On Mother's Day one year, Bubba, my cousin Dale, and I all went out for breakfast. Oddly, we were listening to AM radio station, which is 99 percent talk radio. As we were pulling out of the restaurant, the DJ said, "Because today is Mother's Day, we are going to play some music, and we are going to kick it off with a timeless classic." After the first few notes, I knew exactly what song it was, and I told my cousin "You do know that that song is for you?" He said, "Really?"

"Donna" by Ritchie Valens blared out of the truck radio. His mom, who had been gone some six years, was named Donna. This is one of those "hit you between the eyes with a two-by-four" sign I'll never forget how white he turned when he realized I knew what I was talking about.

CHAPTER 7

My mom had passed when I was quite young, nineteen, and she was only fifty. The loss of a parent can be devastating, but it is even more emotional when you are pregnant and were the worst daughter ever. To explain the "worst daughter" comment, I was a brat. I mean a brat! When I was young, my mom was a stickler for etiquette, and she taught me everything I would need to know, especially about attending church. White gloves for spring and summer, black gloves for fall and winter, white patent leather to match the gloves, and the same with the black. She taught me everything about being a lady, for which I will be forever grateful.

I'm not sure when it started, but I would mouth off to her and say the nastiest things meant to hurt, although I loved her so much. When I reached about eleven, the doctors determined my outbursts were probably a neurological effect from the virus I had had when I was two or three. I was put on phenobarbital, and it did calm down me and my mouth.

My mom had a mental issue, a breakdown of sorts, and after a short hospitalization, she was back on track. She was living in California at the time, so my sister, Myra, and brother-in-law, Pete, flew out to bring her back to Illinois. I can truly say it was wonderful to have her home. We went out and went to dinner, and bingo— real mother-daughter things. She came in September and wanted to return to California before Christmas so she could spend it with her boyfriend. She spent Thanksgiving with my husband and me, my three-year-old daughter, my sister, Pete, their six kids, and my dad. What a wonderful holiday. My in-laws came over, my father-in-law brought his guitar, and we sang. I was silently hoping Mom would change her mind about Christmas, but she didn't.

About a week later, Myra, Pete, and I took her to the airport for her flight back to California. We weren't at the gate too long when her flight was called. We said our goodbyes, and I was last. I don't remember ever hugging her that tight. When she got to the walkway, she turned around and looked at me. I can never describe the feeling, but I knew I would never see her again.

A few days after Mom left, my sister said there was a package at her house for both of us. I put daughter Lori in the car and drove off to Myra's house. The package was our Christmas presents from our mom: portraits, in two different poses. We chose our favorite; my sisters wanted the one of her smiling, and mine was of her not smiling. I never really saw my mom smile much, so that meant more to me.

The next day, I was on the phone with my sister and looking out my window when I saw a new red Ford Thunderbird drive right in front of my house, and I swore to all that was holy my mom was driving! The next day, Friday, December 17, 1971, a letter arrived from her telling me she had bought a new red T-Bird, and she knew I would love it. I tried to call her, but she wasn't home.

That night was the annual Christmas party at the Moose Lodge, and of course Paul would be busy running something. We got home about 1:00 a.m. and went right to bed. A little after 3:00 a.m., the phone rang, and I could hear my sister crying when Paul answered it. I just knew it was my aunt, who had been sick for a while. He hung up the phone, and I said, "Is it Hazel?"

He said, "No, honey, it's your mom. Myra just got the call. She passed a couple of hours ago." I went numb.

God allows us to tie up loose ends now and then, and I knew I had so much more to ask forgiveness for.

CHAPTER 8

In 2012, I lost my sister, Myra, my only sibling. That was a rough one; as I said, there was a ten-year age difference, so when she was twenty, I was a very intolerable ten-year-old, and I drove her crazy—hence my nickname "Queenie" because she felt I was quite spoiled. She was old enough to go out with friends and do things with my mom, so I was jealous, but on the other hand, she was a pretty good sister. She taught me how to roller-skate (which I loved and could do by myself). I practically lived at the Waukegan roller rink. She would take me to scoop the loop and only left me home if there was a curfew. Another activity we enjoyed together was our awesome beach. We would get there early as she got off work from the late shift. We grabbed towels, lotion, and sunglasses and were off. There were huge rocks where we would put out our towels, and both of us would be able to lie out and sunbathe.

She was very talented and amazed me. I couldn't even sew a button on, but in her thirties, she started making her own clothes—and not just pants and shirts. She made formal wear, caftans, and gowns. She also made clothes for her grandkids and for my kids. She was an incredible beader, and she beaded my daughter a belt with her name and a Thunderbird beaded into it. She would bead jewelry, Christmas ornaments, cigarette lighter cases, and more. I do not know how this woman did it with those tiny beads and her incredibly long fingernails. She totally amazed me, and I was very proud of her.

She had always had health problems, with at least ten bouts of pneumonia that I can remember, so her lungs were pretty beat up, which made her very susceptible to any lung infections; the smallest germ could land her in the hospital for weeks. But one thing she didn't lack for was love: her kids adored her, as did her husband. It was a very rare love, the kind one reads about. She was diagnosed with COPD and had made several trips to the ICU. The last trip there, she was admitted to the hospice unit. She had quite an audience in that room. Kids, grandkids, great-grandkids, extended family, and I were in and out her entire stay. It was a terribly hard week, watching someone you love so much slowly fade away from this life. But it was out of love that we stayed, and the doctor said she could hear us, so we kept conversing to her. We were sleeping in chairs, on the floor, or wherever we could lay our heads.

My brother-in-law, Pete, thought at one point we should all go in one at a time to say our personal goodbyes to her. How do you say goodbye to your only sibling? For all the fussing and arguing, I still loved her with all my heart. Needless to say, I blubbered through my entire goodbye. However, I did ask one request of her. We always believed in the secret (the secret being what is on the other side of this life) and what was on the other side of this life, so as I'm crying and holding her hand trying to make my point, I told her how we've always been different. She had dark hair and olive skin; I had blonde hair, and my skin looked like milk. I had curly hair, and she had straight-as-a-poker hair. "Because of our differences I'm going to ask you a special favor when you get to the other side. People are always finding pennies from heaven, however because we've always been different, I want nickels! I will certainly know it's you. I will certainly know you now have the secret."

That night, we had the priest come up and give her the sacrament of the sick. After he departed, we were laughing about some memories, and we thought the best goodbye we could give her was to be happy and laughing with love. We each found some uncomfortable place to sleep that night. I did ask my great-niece, who was sitting next to my sister, to please put her hand on Grandma's chest. We all got a few winks that night, but in the early morning of Sunday, June 17, Father's Day, my niece, who had her hand on my sister's chest, said, "I don't feel anything." We called for the nurse. She came in to check my sister's heart and told us that she was sorry for our loss. My sister had left sometime in the night.

There was so much yet to do with funeral arrangements: mausoleum, priest, funeral home, and so much more. My brother-in-law was still including me in everything, and I did feel quite honored that I was in that family circle. I wrote the obituary, and he included me in any decisions so I didn't feel like a fifth wheel. Those were a rough couple of days getting the arrangements, the priest, and the church. During this time, there weren't a lot of moments for grieving because we were so busy doing things we knew she would want and making sure that everything was as nice as possible.

We all dreaded the wake. That first step into the parlor and to see my sister in repose took my breath away. Even in death, she was so beautiful, and I knew at that moment I would miss her every day.

Later in the evening, the ladies auxiliary from the church had a small ceremony. As they began, I sat down in a chair and looked over. The chair next to me was empty, so I set my purse there. It was a nice ceremony, and several people got up and spoke about a memory they had of her; some funny, some were about her accomplishments, and some were simply a general memory. I spoke up about the time we sent Pete to get plastic water rafts for the pool. The first two lost air right away, so he was kind enough to return them for two more. We got on those, and they too started losing air. My sister was aggravated when these two also lost air, so my kindhearted brother-in-law went back up and bought two more. He filled them with air, and as my sister and I started to climb on them, we looked at each other. We realized with our long fingernails, every time we pulled ourselves up the raft, we were putting holes in them with our nails. She said, "Don't you tell Pete!" Nope, my lips were sealed—until that night of the wake. I'm not stupid!

When I finished that story, Pete was up in the front of the parlor, and I was in the back. Then I hear, "Yeah, well, I know now!" "Yes, you do, and I'm way back here!" When the ceremony was over, people got up and milled around, so I reached over and picked up my purse. On the chair under my purse was a nickel! I knew right then and there she was with me. I smiled and said, "Thanks, Myra."

CHAPTER 9

In the spring of 2013, my daughter Pookie was here in Chicago for some continuing education for her job, so I snuck away to spend a couple days with her in the city. The second night there, our cousin Ron invited us to his boat for dinner. He was docked at Burnham Harbor, and of course not knowing where we were going, we hopped a cab. We figured the cabbie would know where he was going. He didn't speak much English, but we kind of guided him on what little we knew, and finally we pulled up to the harbor. I saw my cousin at the other end of the dock waving at us, and we waved back. We had to walk the length of the dock to meet him, so we got out of the cab, thanked him, and started walking. We went about six or seven feet and then stopped dead in our tracks. I had the spirit bumps so bad it felt like I was a voodoo doll, like I had pins and needles sticking everywhere on my body from the bottom of my feet to the top of my head. My daughter stopped, turned to me, and said, "Mom, somebody is here." I said, "I know." We were both getting every possible spirit feeling we could get standing on that dock. We started looking around because we were on the dock and surrounded by water. What or who could possibly be there to cause these reactions? Remember when I told you my sister and I didn't get on so well when we were young, and she had that facetious pet name for me, Queenie? We were looking around this dock, harbor, or whatever, and I spotted it. I poked my daughter so hard that I almost put her in the water. In plain sight to our right was a boat directly across from us, and its name? *Queen Myra*. We both started shaking and crying because we knew at that moment, my sister (and my daughter's "Annie" (she could never say Aunt Myra, so it always came out "Annie") was with us.

We finally met up with our cousin and had a very enjoyable time eating dinner on his boat. It was a beautiful evening with great company and a soft breeze.

One would think we would have slept like babies, but we spent a lot of the night going over our experience and our interaction with my sister. We did sleep well after that because we had a guardian angel with us.

CHAPTER 10

A few weeks after my sister passed, I was home alone doing my nails. Now, remember, she had very long nails. I had had an accident some years before, and my right hand is quite weak. If my nails get too long, they will undoubtedly break or crack, so I save myself the agony and cut them before necessary. Because of my right-handed weakness, it is very difficult to squeeze nail clippers. These days when I do use clippers, I let the nails fall where they may. When I'm all done, I gather them up and throw them away. This night was no different.

I clipped the nails on my left hand, and of course, they went airborne. I would look for them later. I ran to the bathroom to grab something, and when I returned, this was what I found: all the nails lined up perfectly in a row.

I was home alone that night, and my Bubba was in the hospital. Of course it was my sister, who thought fingernails should be properly cared for!

Many in my family believe that I am half cracked, but I know what know. I love getting these signs because I know love goes on. I wish everyone could get that feeling.

A couple of months after my sister passed, I was at the sleep institute for a follow-up on my sleep study for sleep apnea. The office was a bit busy, so I grabbed a magazine a settled in a chair. I started to hum to music on the overhead, "Somewhere Over the Rainbow" by Israel Kamakawiwo'ole, a singer my sister had seen on one of her trips to Hawaii, and she loved him. He does a beautiful job on that song. It made me smile to myself; yep, she was here.

When I was done and sitting in my car, it dawned on me: there is no music in a sleep institute! They need the quiet for all sleep studies!

CHAPTER 11

Losing Bubba was very hard on all of us. He was such a kind and endearing soul, and his loss was felt for quite a while. I had his two little Jack Russells that I cared for after he passed. They were a handful, but they were so cute. They would sit on the deck at night, especially the little white one, and look through the railing while waiting for their dad to come home. That was what they would do every time he went to the hospital: they would wait on the deck for him to pull in the driveway. The problem was this time he didn't. They were quite depressed for a while, and they kept looking for him for about a month.

It didn't take long for me to start finding pennies. I found them in the middle of my living room floor, or in my bed when I pulled back the blankets to retire. I found one stuck in my pepper spray, so I knew they can only be from him due to the weird spots in which I found them. We had matching rocker recliners, and the one thing that got to my heart was every now and then, mine would rock. Bubba had a habit of going out on the deck to have a cigarette before bed. As he would walk behind my chair, he would kiss the top of my head, which would cause my chair to rock. After he passed, this happened a couple times a week for maybe three months. It was a great feeling knowing he was there.

I have an old school friend who would come and stay with me off and on. I let him have one of the three bedrooms, and he quickly found a job at Ace Hardware. Steve and I had been friends for years; we went to junior high together and had an awesome friendship, and the best way I can put it is that Steve was the brother I never had. He was available for anything. If there was something I wanted to see, such as a movie or show that my husband did not want to go to, I would drag Steve to the venue I wanted to see, and he'd do the same with me. Our last night out was dinner and a Ron White concert, so it was dinner and a show—a date night.

The first date night was rather funny. He picked me up in a AMC Concord that was over twenty years old. I should have just walked back into my house, but I soldiered on. We went to Poplar Creek to see Brooks and Dunn and Reba McEntire. We were standing in line, and he held a very beat-up blanket for us to sit on. I asked him if I could see the tickets. You should have seen the look on his face. He hadn't bought them yet! Fortunately for him, they could be purchased at the entrance. It was a great concert, and I'm not sure what was on his mind, but we were staying friends.

When he got me back to my house, this was how the conversation went. "Can I come in for coffee?" he asked.

"I don't have any coffee."

"Water?"

"Nope."

"Milk?" he tried.

"Nope."

"So I guess juice is out of the question."

I said, "Pretty much."

He called me at work the next day, and a true friendship was born. Eventually he came to work for our company as a business manager. He worked for us off and on and lived with us off and on as well. He had some issues he could never overcome, although he tried. I think his heart wasn't in it.

We had a ritual every day. At three thirty, we took thirty minutes and watched *Jeopardy!* together, and for Final Jeopardy, we would bet a quarter as to who got it right. He was no slouch because he had a bachelor's degree in science and a master's in health-care administration. I think we come out about even on the questions.

He was a great help in organizing the office and kept up with the accounting, taxes, and such. He would do anything for me or my husband, Paul. In fact, he usually spent the holidays with us, or at least the holiday meal.

It was coming to the point where I would have to leave my beautiful mobile home. I hated to because I loved that place, but the rules and restrictions were choking me, and the lot rent was as much as rent on a nice house. I found a house in Waukegan, just five blocks from my husband and our family home. It was a wise choice, and I know it was guided by God.

CHAPTER 12

I had found a house much too big for myself, so I asked my niece and her daughter if they would like to share the house with me. They said yes, and moving day began. My great-niece had two kids, and they were a joy to have around. They were also smart—those two little buggers had it going on! I was moving in the back door, and they were moving in the front. So it began.

My niece, Dawn, was bringing stuff in the front, and she had a piece of paper in her hand. She said, "Aunt Lynnie, isn't this your handwriting?" I took the paper from her and began to read it. When I realized what it was, I plopped in a chair. Dawn asked what was wrong, and her face got very white when I explained to her that it was a letter I had written on my late father's birthday in 1987. This was 2015. That letter had been in a wallet that was soaked in a sink full of water after someone had swiped it. I never saw the wallet again and had forgotten about the letter. Right then, I knew everything I learned, the enlightenment, and signs had all come with me. Once again, I knew my dad was with me. The letter was a bit faded, but I have since laminated it.

The parade of pennies increased, as did the nickels. I found so many in what was still a rather empty house. Dawn told me one day, "You are freaking me out!" The pennies and nickels kept appearing: a nickel and a penny side by side on an empty garbage bag, a nickel on the bathroom sink. I came out of Walgreen's, and next to my car where I had just stepped out was a penny. I can really make a haul at Dollar General; Bubba and I shopped there often, and I can promise three out of five trips will yield pennies. Like I said earlier, I don't look for them; I'm guided right to where they are. It's like digging in my yard: no one is around, and from the dirt, a penny jumps up from the hole! Hello, Bubba.

Still trying to get used to the new house, and then realizing that we really weren't alone, made for an interesting settling in. For instance, we were standing in the kitchen one evening talking, and from the top of the upper cabinet, over the refrigerator, a cooling rack flew off the cabinet, hit the kitchen floor, and slid into the dining room.

We went to Walmart one day, and as I was checking out, I saw a gentleman whom I could have sworn was Bubba. Bubba had had his right leg amputated above the knee a couple years before he passed, and this gentleman was minus his right leg above the knee and in a wheelchair with Harley Davidson stickers on it (Bubba was a biker). He was as bald and fur-faced as Bubba. My daughter was with me, and we both nearly fainted. I happened to see him on another occasion and stop to talk with him. I showed him a picture of Bubba, and he said, "Yep, that's me." Of course he was kidding, I think!. There were many similarities between the two, including his name, Bill, which was Bubba's father's name! See how things fall together?

✠

CHAPTER 13

After the big move, getting used to things, still working for my husband, my niece Dawn had a heart attack. She was so tiny, and I hated to see her this way. She had a successful bypass and was home in a couple of days, however things had been a little tense in our household. We agreed when she said they were moving out. I was so hurt that it didn't work out because I loved them all so much and had only wanted to help, but I also wanted them happy. It sure was quiet with those little ones gone, but God works in mysterious ways. I knew my daughter had been having marriage troubles but did not know how bad. I went by her house one day after my nieces moved out and asked her if she wanted to leave her marriage and live with me. She started to cry, and the next thing I knew, we took what we could grab, my husband brought a van, and she moved in with her two sons and a daughter. This house had five bedrooms, so her kids were so happy! I did not know how bad things were until the kids opened up to me. I know this decision was guided by God.

She was busy getting situated while I put in my last few weeks in our company. By now, Steve had made a sleeping area in our office in the basement, so we were both nearby. On March 1, 2017, Paul, my husband, called me. When I answered, he said, "Steve is dead down there."

I said, "What?' and he repeated it. No, he hadn't called the paramedics, so being only five blocks away, I was there in minutes. I ran down the stairs, and there was my friend, in eternal sleep in his office chair. His battle with the bottle finally over. Twenty years of memories flashed through my mind as I talked to him, waiting for the paramedics and the coroner. That was the last time I ever saw him.

A week after Steve passed, I went in to work, pulled out my chair to sit down, and there it was: a quarter! Yes! My first sign from Steve, and of course it was a quarter! I picked it up, sat down, and started to cry. Of course he would never leave me! As with all my other signs, I felt him close by. Three days later, I was wiping down his desk, and there was another quarter. I had been at the desk several times, and there was no quarter before. The next week, I walked out the back door for some air. I looked down (or was guided to), and there in the crack of the sidewalk were two quarters, standing up on end, side by side. I smiled and said aloud, "Well played, Sparky."

Three weeks after that surprise, my daughter Lori and I were in the living room, folding clothes and chatting. In a moment of silence, we both looked up, (can't say why) but from the ceiling—yes, the ceiling—dropped a quarter. It landed in front of me on the floor, spun around a couple times, and flopped over. My daughter freaked out. Then she said, "How often does this stuff happen to you?"

Laughing, I said, "Quite a bit. Get used to it."

"Yeah, well, you're freaking me out!"

✖

CHAPTER 14

I want to express that this is not something you should look for or be searching for. You will spend a lot of wasted time looking for something that will show itself at its own time. You can drive yourself crazy: "Is that a sign? Is this a sign? Is that my mom?" Signs can be very subtle, and it's usually something that's very close to you or to your loved one that you'll recognize right away. My aunt, for example, always wore Intimate perfume, and whenever I smell it I know she isn't far away.

Also, don't go to disbelieving. It's like a double-edged sword, I guess. For example, my daughter's best friend passed away, and her favorite thing was sunflowers. I told her, "Every time you see sunflowers, that's Kathy." If something happens you are a not sure about, sit down and think about whether this happened in your life before they passed. Is it something they did before they passed? Did they collect things, like angels or glass balls? Then yes. Always be open to whatever may come your way. If you are open, you'll find you'll get signs easier and more frequently. I like to use meditation, but not necessarily sitting there in the lotus position *om*ing for an hour, I like to sit at the beach, walk the pier, and watch my birds as they sit and feed on my feeders. It should be something that sends you into a state of calm or peace. We have beautiful parks in our area and an awesome beach; those too are very good places to get your calm on. Nature is not only calming for the soul. You can learn so much about yourself, the earth, and your inner feelings. Communing with nature is as old as time. I guess that is why it works.With me, after the signs started coming in and I realized what was going on, I started getting what I call spirit bumps. It's like goose bumps, but they get so intense, like thousands of needles. That is a bit painful, but I guess they want my attention because that's what happens.

I'm not sure if you've heard this, but it is said that a cardinal in your yard is a sign from someone on the other side. As I said, I was a pretty hateful kid. I didn't hurt people physically, but I had a rather big mouth and was kind of mean to my mom. My mom crossed over when I was nineteen, and I felt somehow I didn't need to feel bad because I was just a kid. But that's not true. As I got older and further into spirituality, I realized I had to ask her to forgive me. I didn't mean it all, and I loved her, but I couldn't carry this anchor around my neck and heart anymore. I remember spending one night after my evening prayers, saying, "Mom, please forgive me. This is hurting me so much, like I'm sure I hurt you. I'm asking you to please forgive me. I love you, I hope you're at peace, and I hope to see you again." I wasn't expecting a sign right away, so the next day, I went about my normal day. At about 5:30 p.m., I went into the kitchen, and there was a window over my sink. I happened to look up out my window, and there, sitting on the top of the shepherd's hook of the birdfeeders, was a beautiful bright red cardinal staring right at me. I had goose bumps, chills, and a swelling heart because I knew my mom had forgiven me.

I encourage you to read other authors about what the signs are and how spirits affect them. Everybody has a different feeling or premonition of a sign coming on, and you may end up getting your own. Maybe your ears will burn, or your palms will itch. Whatever may become different in your life, be aware of it and think about it, but never be afraid because these are people whom love you and who loved you in this life letting you know that they are okay, they are fine, and they are with you. And don't forget those pennies from heaven—pick them all up. I do!

Love and Light,
Lynnette

EPILOGUE

This book has been a lifelong dream of mine. Not this particular book, but I had wanted to write a book. I had been struggling with the losses of my sister and Bubba. I was taking college courses on divine communication, guidance and prayer, and meditation in spiritual counseling with the American Institute of Healthcare Professionals. I loved what I was learning, but now what? I've said this before: I was guided, and that was how this book came to be. I was alone, and it was February 2013. I was sitting on the edge of my bed ready to go to sleep when this feeling came over me. Don't ask me how I knew, but it was an angel telling me that what I'd learned and experienced should be shared. I should write a book!

You can see this didn't happen overnight, but I never gave up. Everything in this book is truth and fact. Everything I say that happened did. The message is that this happens to all of us, so you should simply be open. I love to see the joy on people's faces when a sign clicks for them. I will never get over the wonder I feel when loved ones let me know they are close.

Since I began the book, there have been so many changes in my life. Although I didn't think it was possible, I am much closer to God. While writing this, I had to relive so many sad things in my life, but that's what God wanted. I have had to say goodbye to my husband of forty-six years, Paul; a great-nephew; a niece; and a good friend and neighbor. But that's the circle of life: we love them, they leave us, and then we meet again.

Now, they all know the secret.

Printed in the United States
By Bookmasters